SEALS & SEA LIONS
A PORTRAIT OF THE ANIMAL WORLD

Andrew Cleave

NEW LINE BOOKS

Fax: (888) 719-7723
e-mail: info@newlinebooks.com

Printed and bound in China

ISBN 978-1-59764-364-1

Visit us on the web!
www.newlinebooks.com

Author: Andrew Cleave

Publisher: Robert Tod
Book Designer: Mark Weinberg
Production Coordinator: Heather Weigel
Senior Editor: Edward Douglas
Project Editor: Cynthia Sternau
Assistant Editor: Linda Greer
DTP Associate: Michael Walther
Typesetting: Command-O, NYC

PHOTO CREDITS

Photographer/Page Number

Innerspace Visions
Doug Perrine 5, 7, 10, 20, 33 (top), 35 (top), 38, 39 (bottom), 40 (bottom), 53 (top), 69, 71

Joe McDonald 17 (top & bottom)

Nature Photographers Ltd.
C. H. Gomersall 51
M. P. Harris 56 (left)
W. S. Paton 47
Paul Sterry 22

Picture Perfect 42
Gerald Cubitt 28
R. Marion 24-25
John Warden 33 (bottom)

Tom Stack & Associates
Michael Bacon 48-49
Dominique Braud 42
Barbara von Hoffmann 46
Thomas Kitchin 6, 31, 44, 64-65
Randy Morse 11 (top & bottom), 35 (bottom), 45 (bottom)
Brian Parker 16
John Shaw 30
Dave Watts 8-9

The Wildlife Collection
Dennis Frieborn 43
John Giustina 32
Martin Harvey 4, 15, 23, 27, 29 (top & bottom), 41, 50
Henry Holdsworth 36-37, 63 (top), 66 (top & bottom), 67, 68 (bottom)
Chris Huss 21, 39 (top), 45
Tim Laman 12 (top & bottom)
Stefan Lundgren 13, 53, 54 (top & bottom), 55
Michael Osmond 40 (top)
Jo Overholt 62, 70
H. Rappl 18, 56-57
Ed Robinson 52
G. Schultz 63 (bottom)
Jack Swenson 14, 19 (bottom), 34, 59, 60 (bottom), 61, 68 (top)
Tom Vezo 3, 19 (top), 58, 60 (top)

INTRODUCTION

The crabeater seal of Antarctica is probably the world's most abundant seal, with a population numbering over fifty million. They feed mainly on krill, rather than crabs, using specially adapted teeth to sift through the water.

Most *people who have visited the coast will have had some encounter, however brief, with seals or sea lions. The sight of what at first looks like a football bobbing in the waves suddenly coming to life, diving, and re-surfacing as a harbor seal staring at the observer with large, appealing eyes will be familiar to anyone who has been out in a small boat around the rocky coasts of Britain or off the wilder shores of Maine. The strange howling calls of basking gray seals are carried ashore with the wind and waves along many western shores in northern Europe. Visitors to the Galapagos Islands will never forget the experience of walking among colonies of sea lions*

which show complete indifference to their human visitors.

Few people have ever ventured out across the Arctic pack ice to see the newly born pups of the harp seals, but the image of the vulnerable, white pup with its huge eyes awaiting the death-dealing club of the sealer is one of the most potent weapons available to conservationists, and has done much to raise people's awareness of the troubled lives of these animals.

Seals are found in all the world's oceans, although they are at their most abundant in the coldest regions. The warmer seas such as the Caribbean and Mediterranean have only a few left, but there is still a chance of a brief encounter with a seal on any stretch of coastline anywhere in the world. Some have even become isolated in fresh water; the Baikal seal lives in a vast freshwater lake far from any other seals, enduring some of the harshest winter conditions on earth.

Playful Galapagos sea lions learn the skills they will need in later life by practicing mock battles in shallow water near the shore.

A Cape fur seal shows the typical pointed nose of the fur seals and the long whiskers used for sensing prey in the water. Streaming eyes are often seen in fur seals and sea lions, as they produce a secretion to protect them from sea water.

THE SEAL FAMILIES

Most people can recognize a seal, even though there are actually thirty-three species in three distinct families. The scientific name for the whole order is the Pinnipedia. This is derived from the Latin for "fin-footed" (or possibly "wing-footed"). This is a reference to their flippers, which are fundamental to their way of life. Within the Pinnipedia there are three separate families. The Phocidae are the "earless seals," of which there are eighteen different species. They have sleek, rounded heads with no ear flap visible on the outside, although they do possess ears and many have excellent hearing. The second family is the Odobenidae, which contains only one species: the instantly recognizable walrus, notable for its splendid tusks and great size. Like the earless seals, it has no external ear flap, but it shares some features with the third group, the Otariidae, containing the fur seals and sea lions. There are fourteen species in this family, all showing external ear flaps.

Adaptations to Life in Water

All of the seals are adapted to life in water, although they are not as fully evolved as the whales and dolphins, which can spend their entire lives in the water. At some stage in their lives the seals must emerge onto land or ice in order to give birth, and many species spend long periods resting ashore each day between spells of feeding.

Their bodies have become adapted to life in water, a very different medium from air. Water is far more dense than air, so a body moving through water has to work far harder than it would if moving through air, although the water supports the body, permitting some structures, such as the skeleton, to become reduced in size. Water conducts heat far more efficiently than air, so a body living in water is likely to lose heat much more quickly. Water contains far less oxygen than air, so a large creature has to find some means of obtaining sufficient oxygen to support it; for the marine mammals this means regular trips to the surface to breathe. Sound is carried through water more efficiently than through air, so it allows communication over vast distances, and seals have good hearing to make use of this property.

Following page: Australian fur seals are restricted mainly to south-eastern Australia and Tasmania and usually gather in large groups on offshore islands. Males are probably the largest of all the fur seals.

A cooling wave washes around a Hawaiian monk seal. It feeds mostly at night on large fish and squid, using its sensitive whiskers to help find its prey.

A young harbor seal emerges from an ice hole by Le Conte Glacier in Alaska. Although the water is close to the freezing point, the seal pup is insulated by its thick blubber layer and quite unharmed by the ice-cold water.

Streamlining

All seals have a streamlined body shape which is most noticeable when in the water. On land, some, such as the huge elephant seals, look ungainly, especially when trying to haul themselves around, but when in their true element, they also show the torpedo shape so well suited for ease of movement through water. All external appendages have been reduced to aid this streamlining, and the fur is sleek enough to allow water to flow over it freely. The head merges with the torso without any neck, and the body tapers gently towards the tail. The body shape is further aided by the thick layer of blubber beneath the skin, which tends to smooth out any structures which may project, such as parts of the skeleton. In water seals are very buoyant, so they do not need special modifications to help keep them afloat.

Movement

The limbs of the seals are short compared with those of most land mammals. It is the bones of the arms and legs which have been most reduced in length, although they are actually very strong and hidden within the body. The bones of the hands and feet, however, have increased in length to form the flippers, which are used for swimming; they are given extra strength by the addition of cartilage and other connective tissues. The sea lions and fur seals use their front flippers for swimming; they are especially long in this family and the claws are reduced, making them useless for grooming but ideal for propulsion. Their hind flippers are also strengthened with cartilage and they have prominent claws on the inner three toes, so it is these which are used for grooming.

Several feedings a day of a high-fat milk fatten the elephant seal pup at an extraordinary rate. It will need all the protection it can get when it ventures into the sea for the first time as an inexperienced swimmer, so a thick layer of blubber, provided by this rich diet, is essential.

An elephant seal pup takes a drink of the mother's rich milk that helps it put on a large amount of body fat each day. Richer than any other mammal's milk, this high-energy food will enable the pup to build a protective layer of blubber before having to fend for itself in the sea.

Unaware of the perils that lie ahead when it will have to fend for itself, a sea lion pup peacefully suckles from its mother on a sunny rock in the Galapagos Islands. The mother is ever watchful for danger and will ensure that her pup is well prepared for life in the sea.

A Galapagos sea lion cools off in a tidal pool. A thick layer of blubber may be an advantage in the Arctic, but it is no help on the equator! Sea lions often bask in places where they can quickly lower their temperature.

In the true seals the front flipper is usually short and blunt in outline, with the digits armed with strong claws. These are a great help when moving out onto land. Ringed seals use these claws to keep their breathing holes in the ice open by constantly scratching at the edges. The Antarctic seal species have generally smaller claws than the Arctic species, but both use their front flippers for grooming. The hind flippers of the true seals are fan-shaped with hair on both surfaces; claws are present in the northern species, but absent in the southern species.

Sea lions swim rather like penguins, sweeping through the water with their long front flippers; the hind flippers are left to trail behind the body. Powerful downstrokes of the front flippers are followed by a more relaxed backstoke, with the flipper rotating at the wrist joint.

When the true seals swim they hold their shorter front flippers close against their sides; there is a slight depression in the blubber below the skin so that the streamlined body outline is maintained. They are propelled forwards by alternate strokes of the hind flippers and side-to-side waves of the tail end of the

Cooling off in a pool helps, but it is also wise for a sea lion to be close to water so that it can easily escape from danger. Cumbersome on land, sea lions are completely at home in the water, where they are much safer when danger threatens.

body, rather like the movements of a large fish. When moving very slowly they may use the front flippers to stabilize the body, and propel themselves forward by gentle sweeps of the tail end.

The shapes of the bodies of the two main families are an adaptation to their different methods of swimming. The sea lions, which mainly use their front flippers, have strong, bulky shoulders and more tapering tail ends, while the seals have stronger muscles in the trunk and slimmer shoulders. As a result of these modifications, the true seals have less mobility on land, moving around with difficulty, mainly by crawling and humping themselves along alternately on the chest and the pelvic region. The sea lions, on the other hand, with their more powerful front limbs, can walk on their flippers, keeping the bulk of the body clear of the ground. They normally move the front flippers alternately, but bring the hind flippers up together in a series of short steps.

Some species can move more quickly by moving the front flippers together, arching the back, and bringing the tail end up more rapidly, but this strange galloping gait can not be sustained for very long. Many species have roughened patches on their flippers to help them keep a grip on rocks or ice and they can reach an alarming speed at times. The Antarctic fur seal can move almost as fast as a person can run, and the leopard seal can wriggle over ice at a similar speed. Photographers should take note when approaching seals on a beach as they may move with greater ease and rapidity than expected.

Keeping Warm

The body temperature of mammals is approximately 98.6° F. (37° C). A body immersed in sea water will very soon lose heat to the colder surroundings because of the greater heat conductivity of water. Humans, like most terrestrial mammals, would be in serious trouble if immersed in water in the Arctic or Antarctic oceans for more than a few seconds, yet the seals do this

The inflated proboscis of the elephant seal looks intimidating, but it probably also serves as a resonating chamber to make the animal's roar even more impressive.

for most of their lives. They have several adaptations to help them maintain a normal body temperature, whatever the water temperature is around them. The most obvious feature is the thick insulating layer of blubber; fat is a poor conductor of heat, so a good thick layer will help retain body heat. Most seals have a layer of blubber of around 4 inches (10 centimeters) thick enveloping the entire body, except the head and the flippers. These areas have other adaptations to conserve heat, however. The blood flow to these parts of the body can be reduced, thus keeping heat within the body. Blood flow can also be reduced to other parts of the body surface when necessary, such as when diving to great depths where the water is much colder.

The layer of fur covering the bodies of seals also acts as a form of insulation, especially on land, when the coat is dry, as air is trapped among the hair fibers. In water this is less effective, as the pressure of the water drives the air out, and if the hair becomes very wet it is even less useful. However, even a layer of water trapped close to the body will act as a form of insulation, as anyone who has worn

California sea lion pups soak up the sun. As adults with a thick layer of blubber, this would soon cause them to overheat, but these youngsters still appreciate some warmth.

One of the differences between seals and sea lions is that the sea lions can raise themselves up on their front flippers. Watched by its mother, a young Australian sea lion gets some practice in this technique.

A harbor seal hauled out on a rock reveals its compact body shape and short flippers. The round head and relatively large eyes are typical of this species, although its colors can vary from very dark brown through sandy shades to silver.

A Galapagos sea lion, troubled by sand flies, shows how versatile and flexible its hind flippers are.

A large mouth and strong teeth are essential to a sea lion; its good eyesight and sensitive whiskers help it find fish, which it can then grasp securely in its large mouth.

a wet suit for diving will realize. It is only when water is constantly streaming past the body conducting heat away that serious heat loss results.

The compact shape of a seal's body is a further adaptation to heat conservation. Heat can only be lost to the surroundings through the body surface, so the more the surface can be reduced, the less heat will escape. In proportion to their volume, seals have a relatively small body surface. Seals are also large animals, so the ratio of body volume to surface area is more favorable to heat retention.

All of these adaptations have enabled seals to exploit some of the coldest and most inhospitable regions on earth. The Weddell seal of Antarctica is so successful that its population probably numbers well over fifty million, yet they can survive where the air temperature is around -100° F. (-40° C) at times, and the only safe basking sites are on windswept ice floes. By contrast, some of the seals, such as the Hawaiian monk seal or the Galapagos sea lion, live in extremely warm environments where the sun beats down relentlessly. They must regularly take cooling dips, and they often seek shade to lie in. Their blubber layers are reduced somewhat and they have a slimmer appearance than some of their polar relatives.

Molting

Seals' hair needs to be renewed at regular intervals, so molting takes place—sometimes quite dramatically. The sea lions and fur seals lose their old coats and replace them with new fur gradually, so the molting process is not very obvious. In the true seals, however, the coat is replaced over a very short period. This necessitates an increase in the blood supply to the skin, which speeds up the rate of heat loss, so they prefer to spend more time out of the water until the coat has been replaced. The giant elephant seals come ashore in large numbers and huddle together to help retain heat. Not only does the coat fall out, but they also lose shreds of skin, so they are particularly vulnerable at this time and may remain out of the water for several weeks.

A breathing hole in the ice is used by Weddell seals to set off on fishing forays; they can dive to depths of almost 2,000 feet (600 meters), where there is little light, and have large eyes to help them find their food.

While molting is in progress the fur of the southern elephant seals peels away in strips. The seals lie packed in large groups on beaches, which become evil-smelling until they move out to sea at the onset of winter.

Elephant seals can remain in conflict over territory for hours at a time, often with serious consequences for both parties. Their teeth are very strong and their chests are muscular to withstand the impact of frequent body blows.

A Galapagos sea lion, highlighted by the setting sun, contemplates a nighttime fishing trip. Its sensitive whiskers enable it to locate food, even in the dark.

Senses

Seals, being hunters, have excellent senses. Their eyesight is particularly well developed, as they spend much time underwater where light levels are reduced. The retina has increased sensitivity to light by having a tapetum, or light-reflecting backing layer, similar to that present in a cat's eyes. It is probable that seals only see in black and white, as their eyes lack the special cells (found in human eyes, for example) which give color vision. At the expense of not seeing in color, they have a better sense of vision in very low light intensities. The lens is almost spherical in a seal's eye, to cope with the refractive properties of water. When a seal is out of the water its eyes have to deal with different conditions, such as very bright light, so the pupil can contract to a minute pinhole to protect the especially sensitive retina. When on land seals are constantly on the lookout for danger, and they assess a potential threat from another seal by its posture and movements, so their eyesight is equally important in or out of the water.

Hearing is well developed in seals, both in water and on land. They are able to locate the source of sounds underwater and can pinpoint them quite accurately. On land many seals are highly vocal, and bulls often use loud roaring sounds to help establish their territories. A large colony of Galapagos sea lions, for example, will produce a cacophony of sounds twenty-four hours a day. Females call to their young, and the young respond with sounds which their mothers can recognize. The eerie howling sounds of gray seals are frequently heard around the rocky coasts of Britain, and the strange grunting and barking calls of the harbor seals are familiar to fishermen on the sand banks in the North Sea. The walrus produces very strange bell-like calls, and also grunts and rumbles when basking on shore. The underwater calls of the Weddell seal can be heard 19 miles (30 kilometers) away; they consist of trilling and chirping sounds and deeper growls. It is thought by some that these are similar to the sounds produced by echo-locating dolphins, but there is no evidence to suggest that seals use echo-location. Their brains do not seem to be constructed in the same way as the more sophisticated brains of the dolphins.

Seals are able to find their food in the dark. Their whiskers are highly sensitive to vibrations in the water and they are able to detect slight movements, such as the disturbance created by a fish swimming close by. Observations of seals in captivity have shown that, when hunting, they push their whiskers forwards; animals which have had their whiskers clipped, or taped down so that they can not move them, are far less successful at locating their prey.

The whiskers are also used on land as a form of communication; if they are pushed forward, this signals aggression. Females can drive off the unwelcome attentions of males by trying to bite their whiskers, which usually causes them to retire. This works for humans, as well, who can use a stick to irritate the whiskers of an aggressive fur seal which looks as if it may attack. It will usually withdraw very quickly in response to this treatment.

The streamlined body shape of a Galapagos sea lion shows several typical sea lion features, including long front flippers, prominent ears, and a bulky, heavy-shouldered body.

FUR SEALS AND SEA LIONS

There are nine species of fur seals, all of which have a luxuriant, thick underfur, a characteristic that led most of them to become the targets of hunters and reach the verge of extinction. Hunting has been banned for most species, or is now strictly controlled, and some populations have recovered quickly to reach their former numbers.

Appearance

Apart from the luxuriant fur, the fur seals have prominent ear tufts and a short tail. They have less blubber than the true seals or walruses, so their necks are more noticeable, their shoulders are large and muscular, and they are more lively and almost dog-like in their behavior at times. As they walk over rocks their feet spread out to the side, but in the water they use their feet to help them

Following page: Two large elephant seals square up to each other on the Falkland Islands in the south Atlantic. Much time is spent in dispute over the ownership of prime stretches of beach, and arguments sometimes end in bloodshed.

A Cape fur seal grooms itself after emerging from the water. They feed mainly on surface-living fish and squid, caught in short forays out to sea from the breeding colonies.

The Probilof Islands off the coast of Alaska are home to large colonies of the northern fur seal. Fur seals have more pointed noses than sea lions and a thick, velvet-like underfur.

Fur seals have a thick, velvety underfur hidden beneath an even thicker outer layer of guard hairs. Males have a luxuriant "mane," which is most obvious when they have dried off on land.

swim. Adult males are larger than females, and can be recognized by their thick, lion-like manes. The snout is distinctive with its square-cut, bristly appearance; males in particular often sit with their heads raised high in the air, showing the characteristic fur seal profile. Their large, dark eyes are pro-

tected by secretions which run down the cheeks, causing oily streaks to form on the fur.

It is thought that the fur seals originated in the cooler regions of the Pacific Ocean, colonizing other areas, including some warmer places, and eventually giving rise to several species. The northern fur seal is possibly one of the best studied of all the seal species. At

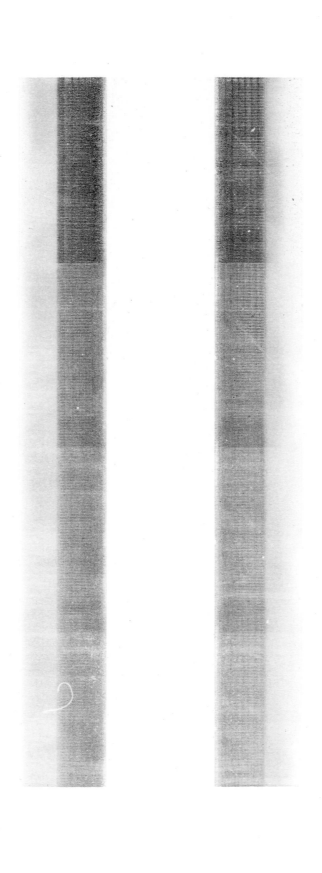

one time it was hunted relentlessly, both at sea and at the breeding colonies, and the population was reduced to dangerously low levels. Now hunting is strictly controlled and confined mainly to young, non-breeding males, and the population seems to have recovered very well; there are even some new colonies being established. They are able to dive to depths of 300 feet (100 meters) in search of squid and fish, and remain at sea for long periods.

The South American fur seal is smaller and less numerous. This seal suffered heavily from hunting and is still recovering slowly.

Several types occur; some are thought to be separate species. The smallest fur seals are found on the Galapagos Islands, where only a small population exists. The largest species is the Australian fur seal, which keeps mainly to offshore islands, so little is known about it. The South African (or Cape) fur seal is also very large and is still relatively abundant, despite centuries of hunting. The young provide the most prized pelts; these are usually taken at about the age of six months.

The Kerguelen fur seal, an inhabitant of the southern Atlantic and Indian oceans and the

Cape fur seal pups await the return of their mothers at a breeding beach. They will soon accompany them out to sea to catch fish for themselves, but will continue to be suckled until the age of almost one year.

*A New Zealand fur seal colony
rests along the rocky west coast
of New Zealand's South Island.*

A large group
of Cape fur seals
plays in the
huge swell
which pounds
the southern
African coast-
line. They are
wary of people
and boats due
to persistent
hunting.

Cape fur seals
inhabit rocky
islands off
the southern
African coast.
They are still
hunted for their
pelts, but the
cull is strictly
controlled and
restricted to the
winter months.

sub-Antarctic islands, was another favorite of the nineteenth-century sealers, so much so that its numbers plummeted to dangerously low levels, but now it has made a very good recovery and is even establishing new colonies. The Guadalupe fur seal is less fortunate, as this species is still subject to attacks by poachers and is vulnerable to disturbance at the breeding colonies. One population lives on Juan Fernandez Island off the coast of Chile, and a more distant group inhabits Guadalupe Island off Baja California. Both Mexico and Chile have passed laws to protect these animals, but their future is not yet secure. The New Zealand fur seal is more fortunate, and the world population, concentrated mainly on islands off South Island and southwest Australia, may be well over sixty thousand. They suffer attacks from Australian fishermen at times, but are otherwise fully protected. In other areas they would be very vulnerable to human disturbance, as they tend to spend most of the year at the breeding colony.

The luxuriant fur of the fur seals looks very sleek in the water. These fighting southern (or Kerguelen) fur seals inhabit the sub-Antarctic islands, where they were once hunted to dangerously low levels by nineteenth-century sealers.

A bull northern fur seal surfaces in a seaweed-filled gully. Much time is spent at sea in search of food, but in the summer breeding season the males return to fight over territory on favored breeding beaches.

The Sea Lions

The sea lions originated in the northern Pacific and gradually colonized the cooler areas of the southern Pacific. They are great rarities in the Arctic, and none at all are found in the Atlantic Ocean. Sea lions have much coarser fur than the fur seals and lack the rich, silky underfur. The flippers are slightly different, with the first digit of the front flipper longer than the inner one. Both fur seals and sea lions can be found at the same breeding sites, but there are several differences in their preferences. Sea lions usually choose open beaches for basking and giving birth, moving away from pounding surf and sometimes traveling quite a distance inshore. They also breed slightly later in the season than the fur seals. Although both are primarily fish eaters, they do not compete for food. The sea lions will usually feed closer to the shore than the fur seals, making far shorter trips out to sea. The fur seals prefer to haul up on rocks where they have easier access to the sea, and in the case of the equatorial species such as the Galapagos fur seal, they nearly always choose a cave or shady ledge to lie on, so they have limited contact with each other.

Steller's Sea Lion

Steller's sea lion is the most northerly of the species and the males are very large animals, reaching a length of 11 feet (3.7 meters). They are quite numerous, with some very large colonies on the Aleutian Islands. Fortunately, their skin is not highly prized, but they do suffer some persecution from fishermen, especially in the western

California sea lions are expert swimmers, a characteristic essential to their survival, and they often use the surf to help them come ashore quickly after a feeding trip.

Steller's sea lions are hunted by fishermen in some parts of their range, so they are very wary if approached by a boat. They often haul out in places such as this, which allow them a rapid escape into deep water if danger threatens.

The fur of a sea lion is rather coarse and lacks the dense, silky underfur of the fur seals, but when it dries out in the sun it has a sleek appearance. Most sea lions show some battle scars, and also look a little ragged when they are molting.

Pacific. There are some well-known colonies off southeast Alaska, and they also live on the Santa Barbara Islands off California. The California sea lion is much smaller, and its main population is centered on the coasts of California and Mexico. Two other types occur, and they are considered by some to be separate species. The Galapagos sea lion, admired and photographed by tens of thousands of visitors each year, is confined to the Galapagos Islands, and the Japanese sea lion is restricted to a few islands in the Sea of Japan. The California sea lion is a very lively and confident species, and is the one most likely to end up as a performing animal in a circus.

The California Sea Lion

The California sea lions have been intensively studied, as the colonies are accessible and the animals themselves respond well to the attentions of humans. The breeding beaches are occupied spasmodically for most of the year, but at the beginning of May the big bulls take up territory and start to gather their harems around them, and the colony then becomes a very noisy place with a great deal of roaring and barking as rival bulls establish the order of precedence. The cows also argue among themselves for the best basking sites and the noise is kept up for hours on end, continuing long into the night.

The pups are born in June in the middle of this frenzy of constantly calling bulls and cows; their squealing cries are added to the rest of the noise, so there is no mistaking the sound of a breeding colony of sea lions. Around two weeks after giving birth, the females mate with the dominant bulls, who then gradually disperse. A few remain on their territory, but many go off to noisy and malodorous "bachelor colonies" at some distance from the breeding beaches. Their main diet is

California sea lions, in common with many marine mammals, were once hunted severely and their numbers declined, but now, with special protection, the population is building up again and large gatherings such as this are much more common.

A California sea lion "kicking out" from a wave while surfing ashore may simply be enjoying itself, or possibly escaping from a predator below the surface. Whatever the reason, sea lions often use waves in a fashion similar to human surfers.

Following page:
A lone Galapagos sea lion resting on a boulder beach displays the large front flipper and the short tail characteristic of all sea lions.

Although the hunting of sea lions has stopped in many parts of the world, there are still many hazards, and sea lions often become entangled in fishing nets. This small section of monofilament drift net is causing a distressing and painful injury to a California sea lion.

A lone California sea lion swims through a forest of giant kelp in search of food; it is fast enough to catch rather large fish, and will also take squid and other marine creatures if it can find them.

Sea lions are normally seen basking in large groups on shore, and below the water they sometimes behave in the same way, keeping together in a large group, and perhaps cooperating with each other to find fish.

Fish scatter in a panic as a group of California sea lions dives in search of food. Several large fish are needed each day to satisfy an adult sea lion.

Australian sea lions scan the beach cautiously before hauling out; this species was once hunted commercially, and fishermen still persecute them for damage to nets, so they are wary of humans.

Sea lions come into their own under the water. They are very inquisitive creatures, quick to investigate anything in their environment. A sand dollar may not be a very tasty morsel, but it is worth a few moments play.

fish and squid but they will try crustaceans and other marine life. The California population probably numbers well in excess of fifty thousand, and in the Galapagos Islands there are around twenty thousand; the Japanese population is very low, with possibly only a few hundred animals remaining.

Other Species

The South American sea lion is a large species confined mainly to the southern half of the continent with colonies scattered from southern Brazil to Chile and Peru. The Falkland Island colonies are probably the best known. They spend much of their time close to their breeding sites, either in the sea fishing or sleeping in large huddles on the shore at night. The Falkland population, despite protection, has fallen inexplicably; elsewhere, due to hunting and disturbance, some colonies have become reduced in numbers, but this is still thought to be a plentiful species.

Two further species occur in the southern hemisphere: the Australian sea lion, which is very large, and the New Zealand sea lion, which is somewhat smaller, although considered by some to be a type of the former species. The Australian sea lion is a very striking animal, with the bulls reaching lengths of around 14 feet (4.2 meters). They have thick coats and massive shoulders. To accompany

An Australian sea lion flees down the beach and dashes into the safety of the water to escape danger on shore. Naturally quarrelsome, they engage in battles with each other and the losers seek the safety of the sea.

their large bulk they have an aggressive disposition and seem to be permanently battling with each other, even when the breeding season is over. Young sea lions have a particularly rough time with adults (apart from their own mothers), who are ready to snap at them and often inflict severe wounding. There may be around ten thousand individuals on a few scattered island breeding colonies. The more docile New Zealand sea lion numbers around fifty thousand animals living in some of the islands off South Island, especially Enderby Island, which has a good colony. In the colder regions, when exposed to winds on their basking sites they often huddle together closely to keep warm.

A shoal of mackerel gives a sea lion a wide berth. A hungry sea lion will take a few, but most of the shoal will be safe. Although fast swimmers themselves, the mackerel are sometimes out-maneuvered by large groups of sea lions.

A bull southern sea lion shows off his massive shoulders and large head with its typical broad, upturned snout. Found around the coasts of South America, these sea lions breed on remote rocky headlands where they are safe from human disturbance.

THE TRUE SEALS

The true seals have no external ear flaps, but they do have ears, and as far as can be judged, excellent hearing. Their bodies are very streamlined and they are extremely efficient swimmers. They are also quite capable of traveling on land, despite the small front flippers. They move rather like large caterpillars, humping their bodies forward, and sometimes using the claws on their front flippers to help get a grip. They prefer to bask on rocks, which allows a quick return to the water, but some of the Antarctic seals occasionally turn up miles from the sea. There are two sub-families of true seals: the Phocinae, which are centered mainly on the Arctic and adjoining areas, and the Monachinae, which are found in warmer tropical waters and the Antarctic.

The Phocinae

The nine species of seal in this sub-family have prominent claws on the front flippers,

which can be used to haul themselves around, and they have claws on the hind flippers, with digits of equal length. They also have three incisor teeth on either side of the upper jaw, and their pups are born with white natal coats.

The common or harbor seal is a small, rounded seal familiar to many people

Ever ready to return to the water, a nervous harbor seal pulls itself over the rocks to the water's edge after having been stranded by the tide.

A harbor seal swims among sea grasses; they prefer shallow coastal waters, sometimes penetrating estuaries and harbors where they catch flatfish on the seabed.

A female harbor seal has hauled out with her pup on a small ice floe below La Conte Glacier, Alaska. They are wary of coming ashore, preferring safer hauling-out sites like this where they can make a quick escape.

because, despite its nervous disposition, it often lives close to the coast where it can easily be seen. They will enter harbors and estuaries and, although they rarely come ashore on the mainland, they will haul out on sand banks, ice floes, and isolated rocks. Two main color phases occur, ranging from pale silvery-gray to a dark or sandy brown. The coat is spotted and is normally paler on the underside. The chubby males are quite active in the water and can often be seen "porpoising" when courting the females. Pups are born in early summer and are able to enter the sea and swim within an hour of birth. This is a special adaptation to their habit of giving birth on sand banks exposed for only a few hours during low tide.

Harbor seals can be found around the coasts of northwestern Europe, with some good populations on the British coastline, and on the coast from Maine to as far north as southern Greenland. There are also a few in freshwater lakes to the east of Hudson Bay, on the Pacific coast of the United States from California to Alaska and the Aleutian Islands, and on the western shores of the Pacific Ocean from Korea to the Bering Straits. Many thousands are killed each year for their skins, or as a fishery control measure, but there may be a total world population of about half a million.

Other Small Seals

The ribbon seal of the North Pacific is familiar to hunters who seek its banded brown and buff coat. It inhabits the pack for most of the year and rarely ventures near land, although it sometimes strays to the Aleutian and Pribilof Islands. The ringed seal is a much more common and widespread species, which lives on the ice of the Arctic ocean.

At only about 4.5 feet (1.4 meters) long, the ringed seal is one of the smallest of all seals. It appears to be very fat and has distinctive spots, which are often ringed, on its dark coat. It is often seen lying on the pack ice, well away from the edge but near a breathing

The "Roman nose" of the bull gray seal emerging from the water is a common sight on the northern and western coastline of Britain where this species has its stronghold, preferring the wilder, rocky stretches of coast.

hole which it can drop into if there is danger in the form of a polar bear or a human hunter. Females dig out snow caverns on the ice to provide a sheltered site in which to give birth; these are sometimes dug out by arctic foxes or polar bears. The world population may be as high as six million, despite the annual slaughter of thousands of pups for the fur trade. They feed on fish, like most seals, but also take large shrimps from the plankton near the surface in the summer.

Two very similar species are the Baikal seal, also very small and restricted to the vast freshwater Lake Baikal, and the Caspian seal, found only in the Caspian Sea. Both are thought to be related to the ringed seal and have evolved through long periods of isolation since the mid-Tertiary period when there were vast inland seas covering what is now Asia. The Baikal seals endure one of the world's harshest winters, surviving under ice ledges and in snow caves, keeping a few breathing holes open so that they can continue feeding beneath the frozen lake.

The Gray Seal

The gray seal is a large animal and most of its population is found around the shores of Britain, with some reaching as far north as the Faroes, Iceland, and Norway. A smaller population lives in the Baltic Sea, and more are found in the Gulf of St. Lawrence and off the Newfoundland coast. Their background

An immature gray seal rests on a bed of kelp which has been washed ashore.

Following page: Harp seals give birth to their pups on pack ice where their main predator, the killer whale, is unable to reach them. This is, however, no protection from human hunters.

color is gray, and the coat is mottled with darker gray in the females. Males have a paler background color with darker mottlings. The "Roman nose" is a characteristic feature of these seals, and it is especially pronounced in the males. Gray seals are quite at home on wild and exposed rocky coasts, breeding on isolated, storm-swept beaches in the autumn. They feed mostly on fish, diving to depths of 320 feet (100 meters) quite easily. The often take flatfish, crabs, and clams from the seabed and will also take commercially valued fish species. This has made them unpopular with fishermen, who persecute them in some parts of their range. Their howling calls are a feature of the remoter parts of the British coastline.

Harp Seals

No seal can have had more publicity than the gleaming white harp seal pup. Public outcry at the slaughter of thousands of these pups, usually by clubbing them out on the pack ice with their mothers watching alongside, resulted from the widespread use of photographs of these appealing animals. Despite the media attention, many thousands are still taken each year for the fur trade. Adult males are relatively small and have a whitish coat with piebald markings.

The harp-shaped cluster of spots on the back gives them their popular name. Females and young are grayer with less distinct harp markings. Harp seals spend most of their time out at sea feeding on plankton and surface-living fish near the edge of the pack ice. In the autumn they move onto the pack ice to prepare for giving birth in a safer environment where killer whales, their main natural predator, cannot reach them. Young are born in March and the males then join the females for mating, after which the colony disperses for the summer. There may be as many as five million harp seals in the Arctic, with the bulk of the population living far out on the ice, well away from the shore.

Bearded Seals and Hooded Seals

Bearded seals are large and lacking in any distinctive markings; their coat is a pale brown above and paler gray below when dry. Most noticeable is the bushy mustache of curly yellow whiskers, used to help the bearded seals locate their food on the seabed. When wet, the whiskers are actually long and straight, and they help the seal to find clams on the seabed. Bearded seals usually lie at the edge of an ice floe ready to drop into the sea if a polar bear gets too close. Eskimo hunters value them for their tough hides, so they are

The long whiskers of the bearded seal help it to locate food in the murky waters of the Arctic Ocean and the Bering Sea.

A harp seal pup rests on an ice floe, protected from the cold by its beautiful fur and blubber layer. The fur, unfortunately, is its downfall, for thousands are killed each year by sealers for the fur coat trade.

very wary of humans and boats. The unusual hooded seal lives far out to sea in the north Atlantic and Arctic oceans, coming to the ice to breed in the spring, and to molt in the summer. The adult males can inflate a sac on top of the nose to act as a threat to other males. This is another species which suffers from hunting, as the pups have beautiful fleecy coats and the adults yield oil and a tough, leathery hide.

The Monachinae

There are nine species in this sub-family, sharing certain characteristics. All have two incisor teeth on either side of the upper jaw and two below, except the elephant seals, which have only one. The two outer digits on the hind flippers are longer than the middle three, and the claws are relatively small. The pups are born with gray, black, or brown natal coats. Some live in warm tropical waters such as the Mediterranean or Caribbean, while the remainder live in the colder southern waters of Antarctica or the southern Pacific Ocean.

The monk seals are a rare and endangered species, reduced to very small numbers through disturbance, persecution, and habitat destruction. They are large seals with dark fur. The Mediterranean monk seal is found in only a few very small colonies and may already be beyond the point at which the population can recover. It is still hunted, despite its endangered status, as is the Hawaiian monk seal, a little more plentiful, but still at a dangerously low population level. It suffers predation from sharks, but also becomes entangled in nets and suffers from disturbance on its breeding beaches. The Caribbean monk seal may already be extinct, as it has not been seen in recent years. It once occurred off many Caribbean islands, but three centuries of ruthless hunting reduced the population to a just a few individuals.

Ross, Crabeater, and Leopard Seals

The Ross seal is a small and little-known seal of the Antarctic pack ice. It has a fairly plain coat with few markings apart from some faint stripes behind the head. It has a

A diving Hawaiian monk seal must learn to avoid fishing nets, which can cause death by drowning. Although it is highly mobile in the water, it seems unable to detect the nets at night when it usually feeds.

The Hawaiian monk seal once lived in colonies of thousands, but, because of relentless hunting, only a few hundred remain, choosing remote and undisturbed beaches to haul out on.

The small Ross seal was discovered in Antarctica during the 1840s, and even today little is known about it except that it shares the remote pack ice with the more common crabeater seals, and feeds on squid.

The most feared of all the seals, the leopard seal, shows off its huge mouth and impressive teeth. The penguin is probably not in danger on the ice floe, but once in the water the leopard seal is its most deadly enemy.

These crabeater seals are at the edge of the Antarctic pack ice where krill is abundant in the summer months. They are susceptible to attacks by killer whales while feeding, and many show impressive scars on their pelts.

comparatively small mouth, and large eyes which appear to bulge when it retracts its head in alarm and gives its curious trilling call. They feed at some depth on squid.

The crabeater seal is probably the most abundant seal in the world; indeed it may be one of the most abundant mammals, with a population approaching seventy-five million according to some estimates. This is a slim, but still large seal with a plain, silvery-gray coat, usually showing the signs of attacks by killer whales.

Adult males may reach a length of 9 feet (3 meters) and the females are thought to be slightly larger. They live far out on the ice, feed-ing on krill, and have specially adapted teeth to help them strain the water to extract their food. The remoteness of their habitat has so far saved them from the attentions of hunters.

The leopard seal has a reputation for feroc-ity and the sight of its vast, gaping mouth armed with sharp teeth does little to discour-age this. It is a predator of penguins, large fish, and possibly the young of other seals. It is a very strong, muscular seal with a strange-ly flexible neck. In water it can easily catch penguins, and with a flick of its head it can skin them by bashing them on the ice before gulping them down. When basking on the ice leopard seals seem to be docile and

The sleek head of a leopard seal emerges from the icy waters of the Antarctic in search of prey.

approachable, but they will move with great ease if threatened and intimidate a human who tries to cut off their approach to the sea. In the water they are curious about objects such as driftwood and small boats and surface very close to them. Shouting or banging on the side of the boat is normally enough to drive them away.

Weddell seals, lying on the Antarctic pack ice, show little fear of humans, and will allow a close approach. Scientists have learned much about seal biology through studying these cooperative animals.

Weddell Seals

Weddell seals are usually found close to land and have quite a different personality from the leopard seals. They allow close approach and can often be touched without waking them when they are basking in the sun. Scientists can attach monitors to them, take measurements, and slip away quietly without the seal showing any signs of distress. Only mothers with pups may be a little more defensive. Weddell seals remain in the water in the winter, keeping breathing holes open in the ice by rasping them with their teeth, which are often badly chipped and worn. They can dive to surprising depths, sometimes going down to 1,969 feet (600 meters).

Protected by a thick layer of fat and heavy fur, a Weddel seal basks on an ice floe in the Antarctic sunlight.

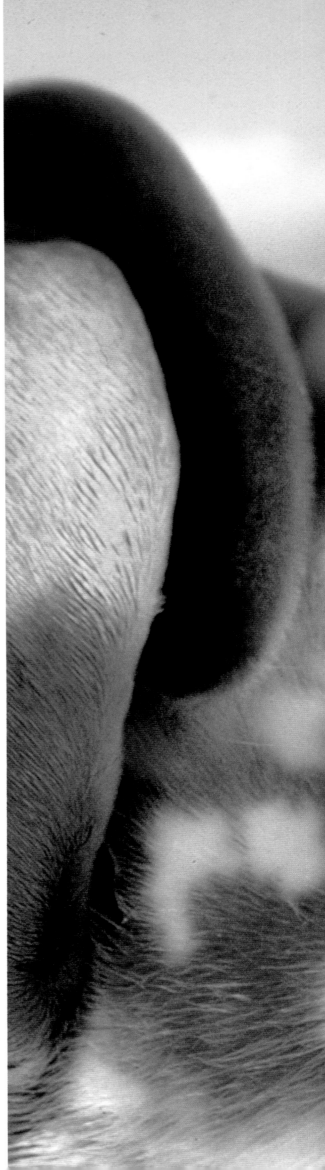

Elephant Seals

The elephant seals are the giants of the seal family, with bulls reaching lengths of up to 20 feet (6 meters). A four-ton (3,636-kilogram) bull elephant seal is a very impressive animal, especially when roaring in defense of his territory. Females normally grow to about 12.5 to 13 feet (3.5 to 4 meters) and weigh considerably less. In addition to their great bulk, males have a pendulous trunk which overhangs the mouth; this can be inflated when the seal is threatening another and it helps to produce the resonating calls used to establish territories on the breeding colonies.

Dominant males take up positions on beaches in December and gather harems around them during the early months of spring. Pups are born early in the year and the males mate with the females soon afterward. After a spell away from the breeding sites, they return in the summer to molt. The northern elephant seal was hunted relentlessly during the nineteenth century and the population was thought to have fallen to as low as twenty seals by the 1890s, but now there may be as many as thirty thousand breeding on islands off California and Baja California.

The southern elephant seal, marginally larger than its northern counterpart, and weighing in as the world's largest seal, is far more numerous. Large colonies occur off Argentina and many sub-Antarctic islands, and they sometimes stray to New Zealand, Australia, and South Africa. Elephant seals can spend long periods at sea and are capable of very deep dives, sometimes as much as .62 of a mile (1 kilometer) below the surface, where they hunt fish and squid.

Because their blubber yielded a rich oil, southern elephant seals were hunted almost to the point of extinction in the nineteenth and early twentieth centuries; now they are recovering and the population once again numbers in the tens of thousands.

A colony of female elephant seals has found a sheltered cove to give birth in. It is important that the young have a secure hauling-out site for the first few days of their lives, as they are not yet fully confident in the water. They are also safe from the enormous bull elephant seals in this secluded area.

The southern elephant seals are the largest of all seal species. They spend most of the winter at sea, returning to land to breed and molt on safe beaches where they spend long hours wallowing.

Exhausted by constant battles, a bull elephant seal rests on a beach, its proboscis showing some of the scars from recent struggles.

The bull elephant seal, the largest seal species in the world, probably earned its name from the grotesquely enlarged proboscis, used here as part of its threat display in an argument over territory.

WALRUSES AND MANATEES

The walruses, in a family of their own, are represented by a single species found in Arctic and sub-Arctic waters. They have no external ear flaps and have lost much of their fur.

Features

Their most striking features are their huge bulk, prominent tusks, and bristly snouts. An adult male can reach a length of up to 11.5 feet (3.5 meters); females are a little shorter. The head is blunt, with a broad, bristly muzzle, and the eyes are tiny, quite unlike the wide, appealing eyes of most of the seals. The ungainly shape and curious facial expression of the walrus makes it the least attractive of the seals to some observers, but on entering the water, walruses become far more attractive and graceful.

The huge tusks are used by males for display, and by all walruses for helping to haul themselves out onto ice floes. It was quite commonly thought that the tusks were used for raking the seabed for clams, and they often appear chipped and damaged as if they have come into contact with rocks, but this is more likely to have resulted from accidental

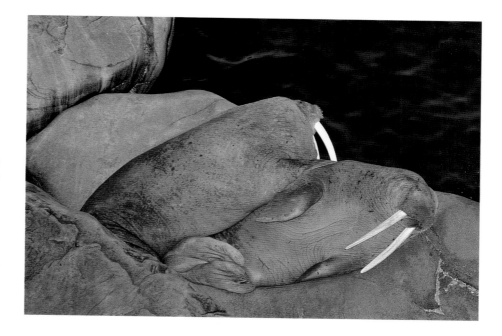

damage while hauling themselves out.

When feeding, the walruses upend themselves in the water, using the tusks to rest on the bottom, rather like the runners on a sleigh. Their sensitive whiskers are able to detect clams in the mud, which they then suck out; they have strong teeth for crunching up the shells and eat a variety of thick-shelled mollusks. Walruses enjoy each other's company and normally haul out in huge numbers at favorite basking sites.

There are two distinct populations: one is the Pacific walrus, living on the ice of the Bering, Chuchki, East Siberian, and Laptev

Basking on rocks out of the water could cause a walrus to overheat, so blood flows close to the surface of the skin to allow heat to escape, giving rise to its red color.

Despite their great bulk and ungainly appearance, walruses are excellent swimmers. They have good flippers to help them reach the seabed and then quickly return to the surface after feeding.

The long tusks of the walrus are a great help when hauling out onto an ice floe, as they give extra leverage to the huge body. They are also used on the seabed when searching for clams for food.

Following page: A densely packed colony of peacefully dozing Pacific walruses on Round Island, Alaska, shows how highly sociable this animal is. They may rest for hours like this, with only an occasional squabble to disturb the peace.

seas. The other is the Atlantic walrus, with scattered groups living on islands and ice floes off Hudson Bay, Ellesmere Island, Greenland, and beyond to Spitsbergen and the Barents Sea. The Pacific animals have rather broader faces and larger tusks. Hunting for the hides, oil, and ivory still continues, although not on the scale of earlier times, and some populations are small and need special protection. Walruses worldwide may number around 150,000, and there are signs of an increase in remoter areas.

When the walrus rests quietly on land its skin takes on a rosy color, hence the scientific name rosmarus. *Once back in the water, the blood flows away from the skin, which reverts to a dull gray.*

The broad, bristly snout of the walrus is an important adaptation to feeding; the bristles help it to locate clams on the seabed in total darkness. It can easily distinguish between edible mollusks and small rocks.

A pair of walruses engage in a half-hearted tussle with their impressive tusks while hauled out on a favorite resting site. The size of the tusks indicates the status of the animal—this pair is evenly matched.

In the cooler air of the high Arctic walruses are less likely to overheat, so when they haul out on ice floes their body coloring remains a dull gray-brown.

A huge colony of walruses hauled out on the shores of Round Island, Alaska, color the shore red for hours on end as they bask in mid-summer. Generations of walruses have used this inaccessible beach, which is safe from predators.

Manatees

Manatees are strange marine mammals, far less agile and streamlined than the seals, and restricted to warm, shallow coastal waters. They have bulky skeletons and thick ribs and skulls. There are no canine or incisor teeth, only grinding molars which move to the front of the jaw and drop out when worn down, to be replaced by new teeth from behind. The tail is large and shaped like a spade, and the fins are flattened paddles with three claws.

There are three species, found in the Caribbean, off the coast of equatorial west Africa, and in the lower Amazon basin. The Caribbean manatee is familiar to visitors to the Florida coast, where around a thousand survive. They are shy, secretive animals with quiet, unobtrusive habits, but a few have become accustomed to human company and have been closely studied. Their tiny, beady eyes are less use than their whiskers when searching for food, which normally consists of waterweeds. They can barely raise their heads out of the water, but may sometimes take succulent plants growing at the water's edge. They are completely helpless on land, so mating, giving birth, and care of the young all take place in water. They are vulnerable to human disturbance, especially from damage by propellers, so they thrive only in areas where they are given special protection. They are sometimes heard to give strange squeaking calls to each other, but otherwise they are very quiet.

A Caribbean manatee and her calf swim quietly through a shallow channel on the Florida coast. Some manatees have learned to trust divers and allow a close approach, although many are wary of humans due to accidents with boats.

Conservation

Some of the seals live in the harshest environments on earth, surviving severe winters and permanent sub-zero temperatures. They are capable of diving deep under the sea, and although not fully adapted to life in the water like the whales and dolphins, they have exploited a difficult environment with great success. Some still live in populations of millions, but only because they are too remote from human influence to have suffered unduly. Sadly, many are threatened, not only by continued hunting, but also by pollution, over-fishing, and habitat destruction. A few species are close to extinction and may not recover even with the protection they have been belatedly offered.

Public outrage at the fate of the harp seal pups did something to reduce the slaughter of these animals, although it still continues, but attention should now be turned to species such as the monk seals, which may not survive beyond the next few years. There should be enough fish in the sea for both humans and seals to take what they need, and the humans, who share this watery environment with these fascinating animals, should take care not to damage it any further before more species are lost forever. The seals, like the whales and dolphins, are able to live in their environment without harming it; perhaps we should learn to do the same.

The rosy skin of a basking walrus contrasts with the algae-coated rocks. Long hours are spent lazing around in the summer, digesting the latest meal of clams.

Its hide coated with green algae, a manatee swims through shallow water in a peaceful Florida creek. Manatees graze on vegetation and live mostly solitary lives, avoiding human activities wherever possible.

INDEX

Page numbers in **bold-face** type indicate photo captions.